Connecticut
Black Business Directory
Volume 1

Created By: Savanda Latrece Gasque

DEDICATION

This Directory is dedicated to all Black Business Owners and Aspiring Entrepreneurs. Your dreams became a reality because you got up and put it into action.

As you continue with your God-given Visions & Ideas remember to:

Trust in the LORD with all thine heart; And lean not unto thine own understanding. In all thy ways acknowledge him, And he shall direct thy paths. Proverbs 3:5-6 (KJV)

ACKNOWLEDGMENTS

Special Thanks and honor to God the author and finisher of my Faith for giving me the vision to begin this awesome project, I'm forever humble and grateful to be one of His chosen ones.

Thank-you to all of Connecticut's Black Business Owners that supported this project, without you I would have not been able to start the 1st Volume of the Connecticut Black Business Directory. I pray for great success in all that you endeavor to do.

Thank-you to all who have supported me during this process, namely: Ingrid Jane Phillip, Takwana Berry-Pipkin, Lysandra Evans-Mendez, Lori Perry, Millicent Dunn, & my loving God-Mother Jeanette Wint, you all have kept me afloat in your own way and I appreciate you all.

BAKERIES

"Satisfy Your Sweet Tooth!"

Ashante's Sweets

Danina Ashante Britto owner of Asante's Sweets is 32 years old she was born and raised in New Haven, CT and currently resides in West Haven, CT. She attended Timothy Dwight, Troupe Magnet School and graduated in 2008 from West

Haven High School, with a 4.0 GPA. Danina became a business owner at the age of 18 but stopped doing business for several years because she wasn't ready to launch. The Business name derives from Danina's Middle name Ashante and she added the word Sweets because she thought that it would be a great fit. In 2018 after praying about her business, Danina took a leap of faith and decided to take it up a notch. When she started, business was slow, and she had very little clientele, but she continued the journey. In February 2020 Ashante's Sweets begin to become very busy with more clientele and her business has been booming ever since. Danina's motto will always be *"BAKING IS MY PASSION and I LOVE WHAT I DO!"* Today she continues to do what God has called her to do and have received many feedbacks and compliments that her desserts are amazing and awesome.

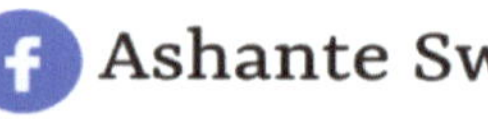
Ashante Sweets

Ashante_Sweets30

ashantesweets.com

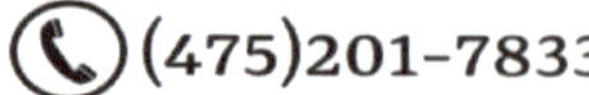
(475)201-7833

PIXIE'S DELIGHTS

Denise Tartt who is affectionally called Pixie, owner of Pixie's Delights has been baking and cooking since she was

8 years old with her mother and father right by her side. Pixie comes from a family of great cooks who growing up used to cook weekly meals for her church family and continued into adulthood for different types of businesses. Denise was asked to make someone a pound cake and from there the orders came rolling in. It was at that moment; Pixie's Delights was formed. Denise loves to cook and bake, and it shows when you taste her delicious delights. All her delicacies are made from scratch and with so much love. In addition to making the cake, you have option to pick-up or have it delivered to you.

 Pixie's Delights

 pixiesdelights.com

 pixiesdelights1@gmail.com

 (860)937-6037

R & S Sweet Delights

Ivy Germayne Kimble owner of R & S Sweet Delights is an awesome baker. She firmly believes that *"THE TASTE IS IN THE CAKE"* and that her hands were anointed to bake and create: *"The Lord shall open unto thee his good treasure, the heaven to give the rain unto thy land in his season, and to bless all the work of thine hand:"* Deuteronomy 28:12a (KJV). R & S Sweet Delights name derives from Ivy's parents Ruth and Sonny. Her father passed in 1997 however, one thing she remembered was her mother always created her father's favorite cakes. Both parents were born in Charlotte, N.C. and were married for over 35 years before his death. Ivy's mother decided to move back to North Carolina after residing in Connecticut for over 50 years. When her mother moved Ivy decided to continue in the mantel of baking. R & S Sweet Delights was established November 2021. Ivy has always had a passion to bake and create. She considers it to be an honor to pick up where her mother left off.

R & S Sweet Delights

igkimble911@gmail.com

(860)794-4472

FOOD &
BEVERAGE

"Enjoy Your Favorite Food & Beverage!"

JUST FISH

Maurice and Takwana Berry-Pikin owners of Just Fish LLC started their business in 2020 at their home in the North end of

Hartford under a small tent. They sold fish sandwiches every Saturday for a month. Every week they added to their menu, the business grew, and the Pipkins decided to open Tuesday-Saturday. It was a God idea to launch out during the pandemic and within a few months they purchased a small food truck. Just like the story in the Bible (John 6:9-10) about the boy who had a bagged lunch with two fishes and five loaves. Jesus took it and was able to multiply it to feed 5,000. Just Fish used the same concept, *"Same hook, different bait"* being mindful of people's situations, the items on their menu are sold at a discounted price. Just Fish's business continued to grow, and they purchased a larger food truck that they currently operate Tuesday-Friday Downtown Hartford and Saturdays in the North end of Hartford. Just Fish hired a small staff and now have a full seafood menu. In 2022 Just fish purchased a bus to accommodate customers, fairs, and larger events and is now opened Thursday-Saturday on Main Street on the North end of Hartford. The Pipkins quotes: *"We are not just another seafood business, but we're building a brand!"*

NO PORK ON DIS FORK

Brian Perry owner of No Pork On Dis Fork LLC started the business on June 2, 2020 after losing full time hours as a cook on his job. At the time he was receiving $600 a week in unemployment. Brian's wife was out of work as well, so he knew he had to do something. He had a choice to make go back to what was familiar to him, go back to the streets, or fulfill his dreams of being an honest business owner.

Brian's dad and cousin owned food stands in Quincy, Mass. And they used to tell him how successful they were in business. He knew that becoming a business owner was the way to become self-sufficient and make his family proud at the same time.

Brian was on Federal Probation when he started No Pork On Dis Fork LLC, as of today he is no longer on Federal Probation. Since the 2020, Brian has been successful in selling Hot Dogs that doesn't contain pork, from his Food Cart in various locations in Hartford and caters community events.

Comfort Kozi Teas was established in August 2020 right at the height of a worldwide Pandemic. The motivation and need for people to have intimate and safe spaces to celebrate events and moments is what inspired Maxine Nugent to start her lifelong dream of a tea business. Maxine dedicates her tea business to her Mum. As a little girl she grew up with her Mum telling her "Maxine go drink a little cup of tea", whenever she had any ailments or just not feeling well. Drinking tea has become second nature and now her dream is to spread the wonders of tea and its comforts to as many people as she can.

• • • • • • • • • ● • • • • • • • • •

Comfort Kozi Teas mission is to provide every customer with an amazing experience. There is more to tea than people may understand, that is why we provide not only a good cup of tea, comfortable atmosphere but also educate on the history and etiquette of drinking tea, while leaving a good lasting impression.

Tea is classy and a fun way to bring people together in a social setting, having them dress sophisticated all while providing a regal experience is what we call the "Comfort Kozi Teas Way". From Sorority meetings, bridal showers, women empowerment luncheons to special moments between a father and daughter, Tea is the perfect connection.

• • • • • • • • • ● • • • • • • • • •

Tea comes in many varieties and flavors and is a beverage that you can drink either hot or cold, but its benefits go far beyond refreshments. There is plenty of research showing that drinking tea can provide comfort and has been used and recommended as a soothing, cleansing and relief for many health conditions.

Nothing better than a great cup of tea!

FASHION

"Creativity At Its Best!"

Fallon & Farren African Wares

Susan Barlow-Pruitt had two goals when she started her business selling authentic African clothing and jewelry five years ago. She wanted to shine a spotlight on the dramatic, colorful Afrocentric styles she loved, but even more than that, she wanted to provide an outlet that gave her twin daughters the chance to learn and develop. Fallon & Farren have intellectual disabilities, and Susan wanted to give them a real-world opportunity to develop skills that would serve them throughout their lives.

With the business that now bears their name, they are learning about responsibility, handling money, and dealing with the public. "It's a great way for them to connect with people," said Susan. "They are coming out of their shyness." Fallon & Farren African Wares has been flourishing for five years. They've attracted customers from near and far, including many parents of children with special needs. Susan says that these people in particular enjoy shopping with her, because it gives them hope that their children could achieve something similar. Before the pandemic, they operated mostly from pop-up locations where they could set up their wares temporarily, but when things shut down, they moved to doing business from their home by appointment only. The transition was smooth, and Susan says that business has been steady. They've even started doing Zoom sessions in which they present their items virtually to potential customers.

Jane's Crafts

Jane Kendrick is the owner of Jane's Crafts, a small business in which she sews and make custom made items. Jane also customizes items with holiday themes, sports themes, and for special occasions. Customers often rant and rave about how much they love their items from Jane's Crafts. Jane uses social media to promote her items and on any given day, you can  expect to see a video of her working diligently on crafts to ship out to her customer.

Email: janecrafts17@gmail.com
Phone/Text: (203)583-8188

 Jane's Crafts

 www.etsy.com/shop/craftsbyjanek

HAIR
&
NAILS

"Selfcare Is The Best Care!"

Pampered By J

Justice Conaway is a nail tech who specializes in the care and growth of natural nails and feet. She uses the best products that are recommended when applying acrylic, hard gel, forms, and gel-x on nails. Justice envisions working with magazines and brands in the beauty industry in the near future.

Pampered by J
justiceconaway@yahoo.com

Norris Barbershop

Norris Barbershop was est. in 1964 by Norris Graves and is presently operated by his son Marcus A. Brown. Marcus is a remarkable man that has a passion to continue the family legacy that was created by working countless hours to keep the business afloat. He is known by his affectious smile and interaction with his customers. When walking into Norris Barbershop there is never a dull moment it's a friendly atmosphere full of love and great conversation. Norris Barbershop has three awesome barbers including Marcus and he continues to inspire and hire Licensed Barbers to expand their team.

Tizzle's Hair USA

Thelma Ekeng is the owner of Tizzle's Hair USA an online business that sells 100% Virgin Human Hair Wigs. Authenticity, excellence and integrity are their core values. Tizzle's Hair USA uses virgin human hair wigs that are made from the best quality human hair.

www.tizzleshairusa.com

Photographers
&
Videographers

"Capture Your Special Moments!"

Favor Photos by M.R.H LLC

In 2012, Margaret Rochelle Hagins started taking photos with her Samsung phone at Prayer and Praise Fellowship Inc. She took  photos for a wedding, baby baptism, and church services then uploaded the photos on the church's social media page. One day Margaret saw a girl with a camera at the YMCA, she asked her the name of it and ordered one. After Margaret received her camera, she officially became a photographer in 2013. While sitting at her desk working at the YMCA she pondered on what she would name the business. Margaret and her friend talked and prayed about it. One thing she always remembered was being told that she has favor from God. The next time Margaret saw her friend she told her that God gave her the name of her business. In the beginning Margaret named the business Favor Photos and then God told her to add the initials of her name to it. The business name is now Favor Photos by M.R.H. Margaret is passionate about capturing your special moment and it shows in the photos.

~We Do More Than Take Photos,
We Tell The Stories Behind The Photo~

"LET US TELL YOUR STORY!"

Margaret Rochelle Hagins
Freelance Photographer
Phone: (860)840-2915
Website: www.favorphotosbymrh.com

BEYOND THE LENS PRODUCTIONS

Beyond The Lens Productions all started when Justice Conaway was in high school. She was interested in doing carpentry but instead chose the Media Production Class. Justice's teacher informed her that she was one of his best students. This compliment inspired her to pursue a career in filming and photography. Justice started her business as a Photographer and videographer because she enjoys capturing stories that is beyond the red carpets and flashy lights, the raw, nitty-gritty, the real stuff that's beyond the lens.

ANOINTED HANDS PRODUCTIONS

Anointed Hands Productions is a video production company started by Savanda Latrece in January 2003, when she became the host and producer of her television broadcast called "Keepin It Real" at Hartford Public Access Television. Savanda was mentored by Pastor J. Stan and Nyeisha McCauley, they encouraged her to perfect her craft by filming and working behind the scenes on other broadcast that was being aired at the Television Station. She learned how to edit, add graphics to the videos, create intros and outros, set the lightning, mic the guests, and many other things that was a part of the video production. Eventually, Savanda started filming local events for a small fee. She is always excited to work with others and loves to see their smiling faces.

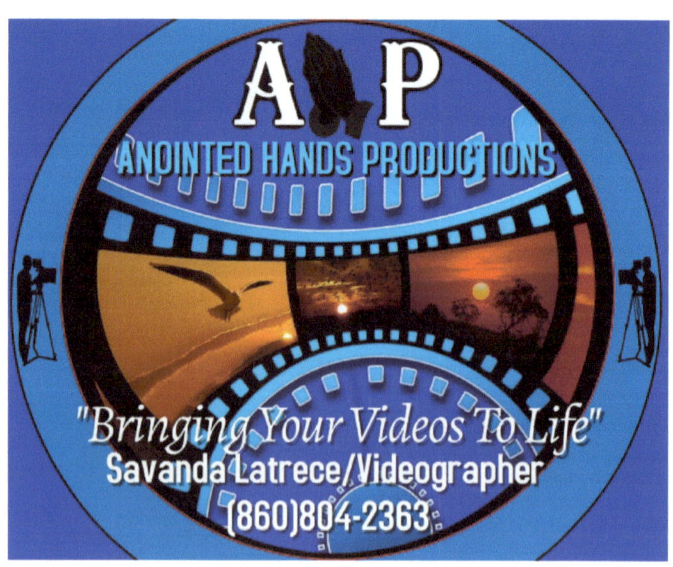

Barkel Mcclane Photography

Barbara McClane is a passionate Connecticut based photographer who connects, captures, and creates meaningful memories of families, friends, pets, and loved ones. Barbara believes that the perfect photography captures the energy that is felt through the camera viewfinder and connects her to the subject. Barbara has worked as a Mental Health Assistant with the CT Department of Mental Health and Addiction Services for over 16 years. In that capacity, she has dedicated herself to caring for, training, and assisting folks with daily life skills. A mostly self-taught photographer, Barbara has channeled her commitment to social justice and humanity into creating art that showcases the complexities and beauty of the  human experience. Her recent projects have focused on highlighting members of her local LGBTQ+ community, and people of color. Her more recent photography projects include:

- "LGBTQ Pride Stories of 2021" (2021)
- "History Makers Now" (2021)
- "Dope Dads" (2021)
- "I am Woman" (2019, 2021, 2022)

"HIS Project: History Impactful Story" (2019, anticipated 2022)
Barbara is also the author of a memoir titled "Blessed, Not Bitter". The book details her personal journey from surviving addiction, prison, physical and sexual abuse to reconnecting with her biological family and inspiring others to find the joy and hope in life. Barbara is the recipient of several awards, including the "2022 Nomination for MLK Award at Connecticut Valley Hospital, 2021 100 Women of Color" and the "2021 Working Women in Networking Business".
Barbara resides in Cromwell, CT with her wife and their two cats.

barkelmcclanephotography.com

C. TJohnson Photography

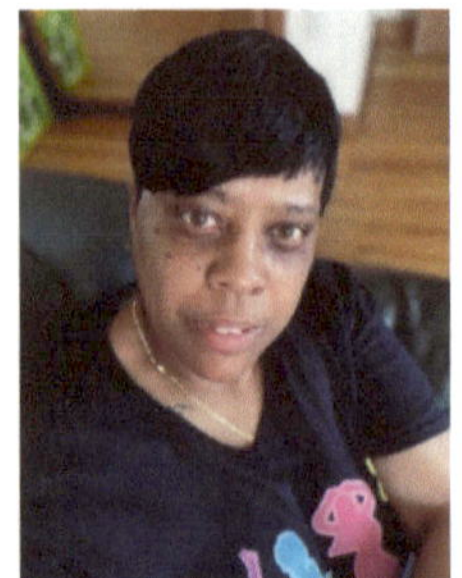

C. Tjohnson Photography is a business that specializes in photography and videography. Crystal Timmons Johnson owner & lead photographer is always excited and ready to capture your special moments.

Mucks Photos LLC

Brian Evans is a 17 year old aspiring photographer. Born and raised in Hartford, CT, his goal is to expand his photography business. Brian's true passion is capturing the best life moments through photos.

HEALTH
WELLNESS
FINANCES

"Your Well Being Is Important!"

Restart My Life Coaching Services LLC

Lori Perry-Williams is an Entrepreneur, Certified Life Coach, Motivational Speaker, Ordained Elder, Author, and Writer. She is the 7th of 8 children born to Edgar and Leora Perry, a dedicated wife to: Edward Williams, a mother of 5 children who she successfully raised in a drug infested project environment, she has 23 grandchildren and 1 great-grand child.

Lori is passionate about empowering the community. She served as a commissioner of Governor Rolland Blue Ribbon Welfare Reform in 1995 and in 1997 she assisted Thelma Ellis Dickerson/Founder of Jumoke Academy in starting one of the first Chartered School in the North end of Hartford, CT.

Lori is the author of two books: "Restart" and "Restarting The Family". She is the host/producer of a weekly podcast called "The Shoe Shop". Lori has three businesses: "Glorious Care LLC", "Restart My Life Coaching Service LLC", and "Lori's Kitchen, LLC.

As an ordained Elder and Evangelist Lori is committed to God and enjoys doing outreach ministry. She has been a pillar in her current church: "For His Glory Church Ministries, Inc." under the leadership of Pastor Suzette Myles for 21 years serving in many capacities.

She is the visionary of "God's Glorious Gathering" an endeavor that was held October 08, 2022, at the Connecticut Convention Center Downtown Hartford that brought together people from around the world for a day of Prayer, Praise, and Worship. Lori continues to be a beacon of light to others by being transparent, sharing her experiences, and testimonies of survival. She is genuine and is an asset to her family, church, business, and community.

Keeping Kids Out Of Prison

Ruben Johnson Santiago is the Founder of Keeping Kids out of Prison LLC., he is an aspired Men's Empowerment Motivational Speaker and currently also works for CT Bail. This was brought into existence by the many Trials he faced as a young man growing up when all he had to look up to, was the love he received from the streets. He is a product of the foster system, older brother of Four, endured Fourteen Foster homes before being adopted at the age of nine. His biological mother became victim to the drug epidemic and contracted the HIV virus and succumbed to her death in 1994. Mr. Santiago spent a total of 12 years in and out of a Federal Correctional Facility finally being released in 2008. He was paroled three  years early on good behavior and has since became a productive citizen within his Family, Home, and Community. He encourages young men to never give up on their Dreams, or goals but most importantly on themselves. No matter what they may be facing at the moment the situation is only temporary and a stepping stone towards their greatness. He hosts Young Teen, and Men Vision Board parties, and host events embarking and discussing serious issues within the youth coming up with ways to keep them off the Streets and "Keeping Kids out of Prison". He also hosts a yearly free Christmas Toy Drive in the New London community in the month of December honoring his 16-year-old son who passed away from Brain Cancer June 21, 2011. He now works with CT Bails out of New Haven, CT bonding inmates out of prison, helping them transition into society and is working collaborations with other community male activist.

Exemplify to Edify, LLC

Miosotys Santiago is a Wife, Mother, Grandmother, and the founder of Exemplify to Edify, LLC. An organization in Groton, Connecticut that focuses on healing with a Faith driven walk with Purpose. She is an Inspirational Speaker, Advocate, Facilitator who focuses on healing through writing, and transparency. Her mission statement is "Your Pain Becomes your Purpose" and she believes that to be true. Mrs. Santiago has a passion, and mission to use her victories, perseverance, and resilience to be used as a tool to help others heal. Mrs. Santiago host Teen, and Women's Self-care workshops (Vision Board parties), has spoken in several School systems in Rhode Island, and Connecticut. Mrs. Santiago has hosted Women, and Teen Empowerment self-developing workshops focusing on, and discovering deep talents that may be hidden underneath the surface of fear, shame, or self-rejection through writing. She an author of her very own Memoir "GOD'S DIAMOND". She is currently a Graduate of the Chamber of Commerce of Eastern Connecticut Leadership program class of 2022. The Director of Outreach at her church home, the Secretary with the Youth Advisory Board with the city of Groton, Connecticut, and a silent member with Safe Futures a Woman's & Children's Domestic Violence Shelter.

Exemplify To Edify LLC

exemplify2edify.org

(860)574-1982

<u>The Godiva Experience Thee HOLISTIX WAYY OF LIVING</u>

Tanesha Shuler is the founder and owner of The Godiva Experience Thee HOLISTIX WAYY OF LIVING, a business that focuses on health and wellness.

The Godiva Experience Thee HOLISTIX WAYY OF LIVING mission is to provide everyone with the best holistic alternative and balance as well as feed their craving of spiritual growth. The service provided is designed with you solely in mind. Whether it's a custom jewelry piece, meditation sessions, essential oil mixtures for needs or alternative diets. They will take the necessary steps as well as time to figure out your needs.

The Godiva Experience Thee HOLISTIX WAYY OF LIVING was inspired in 2020 during Tanesha's pregnancy as we experienced a pandemic, that left us limited resources. So many people were battling mentally and physically with health issues. During that time, it resulted into some having to use nature as that resource. So, Tanesha thought about the near future and how would we survive. It is by living off the earth's resources, it's the most holistic way of life!

 godivaexperience

 godivaexperience08

 The Godiva Experience Thee HOLISTIX WAYY OF LIVING LLC

BLACK CLASS ENTERPRISES

Erika Roberts is a Hartford, CT, native who is passionate about making a positive impact in her community and the neighborhoods where she grew up. As a result, she's spent her career working for nonprofit organizations that help at-risk youth. In 2017, she found her passion as a youth mentor and advocate for Compass Youth Collaborative where she helps youth navigate day-to-day challenges

and build the skills, they need to become successful adults. Erika relates to some of their struggles having overcome similar obstacles, and she works hard to serve as a role model and inspiration.

Engaging with young people who remind her of her younger self has changed the course of her career and given her a greater sense of purpose. What she loves most about being a mentor is giving youth a sense of direction by raising their expectations while promoting peace within the community. Erika founded a consulting business — Black Class Enterprises—that focuses on developing mindfulness, intentionality, compassion, and determination in urban teenage girls.

Erika also makes time for traditional African dancing and drumming. She learned to express herself through dance and drum under the tutelage of Sankofa Kuumba Cultural Arts Consortium.

Erika Roberts

queenme_erikaj

firstclass2st@gmail.com

Hillary Brown

HONEY
B
MARRIAGE | FINANCE | SUPPORT
COMPROMISE | SUBMISSION
Relationship Corner
TUESDAYS 8PM
You Tube
A DISCUSSION ON TOPICS ALL THINGS RELATIONS

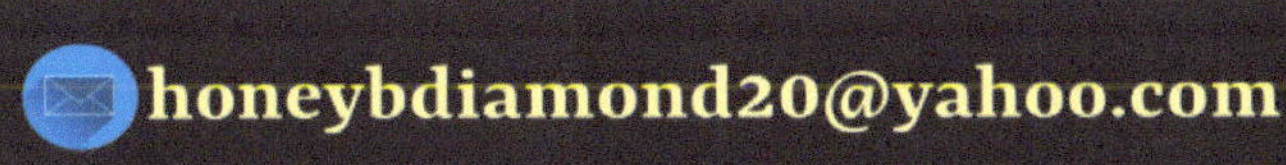

honeybdiamond20@yahoo.com

LICENSED LIFE COACH

Octavia Lockhart-Harris is a licensed life coach who specializes in mindset change. Helping a person to create a strategic plan for a different lifestyle. She helps you slowly build your confidence in areas of your life you may feel your stuck in. Octavia has a wealth of knowledge and wisdom from own personal life experiences that she uses you to navigate through life's challenges. She is always open to new ideas and is willing to do whatever it takes to help you accomplish your goals and dreams. Octavia's warm smile and pleasant attitude makes it easy for those who are going through difficulties feel comfortable to share their deepest thoughts and concerns.

Octavia Harris

harrisoctavia10@gmail.com

(860)268-5739

TASHA ROSE

www.Letstalkaboutitcounselingct.com

Tasha Rose is the owner and CEO of Let's Talk About It Counseling Services. She provides transformative counseling to women 30 plus. Tasha specializes in healing the whole person using scripture, prayer and humor infused with clinical techniques; causing you to have an out of body experience and a positive outlook on self and life.

Healing with: Forgiveness
Accountability
Intention
Transparency
Help

Tasha is passionate about helping women heal. Working with Tasha you will learn how to be transparent, real, brave and face our fears. Breaking down and releasing shame, guilt and unforgiveness worn as a badge of honor. While working with her you will feel affirmed, assured, unchained, safe and inspired to change with love and forgiveness.

For His Glory Church Ministries, Inc. (FHGCMINC), is a nondenominational Sabbath church, founded in September of 2001 by Pastor, Dr. Suzette M. Myles. FHGCMINC was birthed through a prayer group called

Shackle Breakers, founded by Pastor Myles in 2000. Through the power of shackle breaking prayer, the ministry grew in size and impact, branching out and birthing more

ministries including a fully accredited bible college. At FHGCMINC., we believe in 'The Great Commission' of Christ Yeshua (Jesus) to go forth and make disciples of all men (Mark 16:14-18). It is our job as disciples of Yeshua The Christ to reach the lost at any cost and to go to those that are in need of a physician (Matthew 9:12-13). We are to give food to the hungry, drink to the thirsty, clothes to the naked, and visit the sick, the imprisoned, and the shut-in (Matthew 25:34-40).

We believe in healing the sick and casting out devils in the name of Yeshua (Matthew 10:1) (Mark 16:17-18). We believe in keeping the full Word of Elohim (God) which includes all eleven of His commandments (Exodus 20:1-17) (John 13:34-35). We honor the fourth commandment which is to keep the Sabbath day holy unto Elohim (James 2:10) (Exodus 20:8-11) (Exodus 31:12-17)

(Matthew 19:17). We believe that marriage is holy and honorable to Elohim and that anything other than one man and one woman joined together in marriage is a sin against Elohim (Hebrews 13:4) (1 Corinthians 7:2-3) (Romans 1:25-28) (Genesis 2:20-25). We believe in fellowship with the Body of Christ (Hebrews 10:25) (1 Corinthians 12: 12-27) (Romans 1:12). We believe that it is our job to keep the bond of peace in the Body of Christ (Ephesians 4:2-4). We believe that we are to help one another where we see the need (Matthew 5:41-42) (Hebrews 13:16) (Philippians 2:4). We believe in the importance of the true Word of Elohim (Hebrews 4:12) (Matthew 4:4) (Isaiah 55:11). Every disciple of Christ Yeshua must study to learn how to rightly divide the Word of truth (2 Timothy 2:15) (Psalm 1:1-3).

PO Box 254
Hartford, CT 06141

office@fhgcminc.org

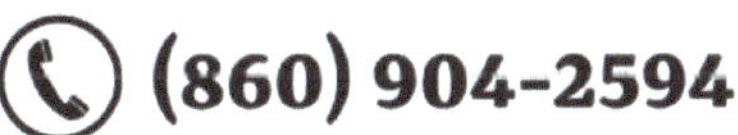

www.fhgcminc.org

(860) 904-2594

ERSKINE ALEXANDER, LMSW (CT)

Human Services-Board Certified Practitioner

Erskine Alexander is native of Columbus, Georgia. Erskine graduated from Carver High School in 1995 with a band scholarship to attend Morris Brown College in Atlanta, Georgia. Erskine graduated from Morris Brown College in 1999 with a Bachelor of Science degree in Psychology with a 3.8 GPA and various academic honors. While studying at Morris Brown College, Erskine's notable achievements include interning at the South Atlanta Psychological Health Center for  Children and Adolescents suffering from ADHD (Attention Deficit Hyperactivity Disorder) and various behaviors disorders. Erskine also interned at Crim High school in Decatur, Georgia working with adolescents in career development.

After, graduating from Morris Brown College, Erskine was accepted into the prestigious Columbia University School of Social Work Master's Program in New York City. He graduated from Columbia University in 2001 with academic honors with notable achievements while attending Columbia University including interning at Friends of the Island of Academy (F.O.I.A) in Manhattan where he worked with young adults and adolescents being released from New York's Rikers Island Correctional Facility. While interning at F.O.I.A, he was able to attend the trial for Mr. Sean "Diddy" Combs for his 1999-gun charge in which he was able to meet the late Attorney Johnny Cochran. Also, while interning at F.O.I.A, he was able to meet the actress Rosie Perez from the movie "White Men Can't Jump and Spike Lee's "Do the Right Thing". Erskine wrote a grant concerning the needs and challenges of at-risk youth in New York City in which the grant was accepted by Ms. Perez resulting in her becoming a partner for F.O.I.A.

After graduating from Columbia University in 2001, Erskine was offered a position to work in the Department of Psychiatry at Montefiore Hospital in the Bronx, New York as a Clinical Care Manger working with client with alcohol and substance abuse problems. Erskine has been working at Montefiore Hospital for approaching 20 years of service. Years. Erskine has worked with over 1,000 clients in the Bronx and Manhattan throughout New York City by assisting them with employment opportunities and Social Security Benefits. Erskine also worked in the Supporting Healthy Marriage Program at Montefiore Hospital where he worked with couples in ways to prevent harmful fights, staying close, managing stress, fun and play, and compromising in the relationship. Erskine also runs behavioral groups and individual therapy sessions for teenagers and adults at risk in the Bronx, New York at Santa Cecilia Inc, **Healing Springs Wellness based out of Cheshire, Connecticut,** and SOBRO based out of Harlem, New York as a social worker being in service for over 10 years of service. Erskine enjoys all job responsibilities and considers it a gift to work with various populations.

Erskine is also an actor in New York City. His film credits include being featured in the amazon films "Somnium" "6 Tales of Sin", and Me Familia 2 directed by Joe Cinemera. Erskine also featured on the television series "For Life" on ABC being executive produced by Curtis "50 Cent" Jackson. Erskine is currently filming for the upcoming film "The Homewreckers Club and "Boss, Kings, and Queens scheduled for release in 2022.

Erskine Alexander

ealexand477@gmail.com

healingspringswellness.com

(646)335-5263

We are accepting New Clients

HOMEMAKER & COMPANION SERVICES

"Dedicated To Providing Optimal Care For Our Clients"

Latisha Anderson & Merva Dixon /Managers

E-mail: devinehomehealthcare1@gmail.com

Phone: (860)255-8307

Types of Payments Accepted
(Credit/Debit Cards, Certified Check, or Money Order)

Please Note We only accept Private Insurance at this time

FOR PROFIT

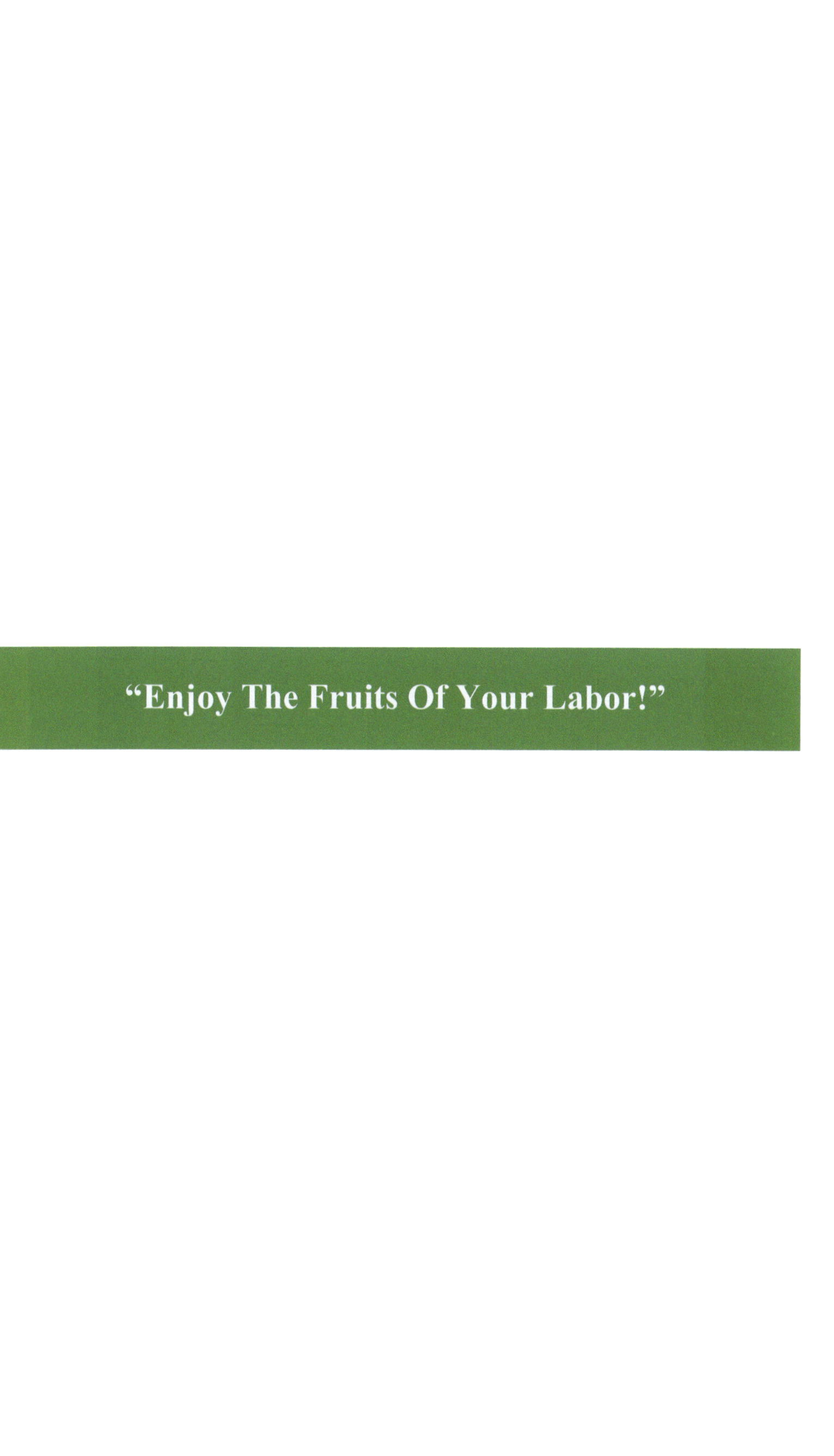

"Enjoy The Fruits Of Your Labor!"

MY SERVICES

POWER STRATEGIST - CONNECTOR - PUBLIC AFFAIRS SPECIALIST

STRATEGIC CRITICAL THINKING CAPABILITIES ADVISOR

COMMUNICATIONS & MEDIA GURU - INTERNATIONAL RELATIONS EXPERT

FOREIGN POLICY NEWS ANALYST - GHOST AND SPEECH WRITER

AWARD-WINNINGNG JOURNALIST - EVENT PRODUCTION MAVEN - HANDLER

GLOBAL CROSS-CULTURAL CONNOISSEUR LEADERSHIP ADVANCEMENT FACILITATOR

TEAM BUILDER TRAINING ARCHITECT ART OF WAR NEGOTIATOR PROBLEM SOLVER

TV & EVENT HOST, MODERATOR & SPEAKER - AU FAIT WORLD TRAVELER

CONTACT

yvonne@davisworldtraining.com

CHOOSE WHAT YOU NEED
THE SET-UP
Maxiumizing Your Potential In:
-BUSINESS -MINISTRY -RELATIONSHIPS
& WE'LL SET YOU UP!
-NonProfit/For Profit Business Formation
-Websites -Flyers -Business Cards -Videography
-Write & Publish a Book -Event Planning -Job Coach
-Customer Service Training -Public Speaking
SAVANDA LATRECE/SPECIALIST (860)804-2363

Author & Writer

Cheryl L. Baldwin had a difficult time in school, which affected her self-esteem and confidence. At Ben Bronz Academy, where she attended, she learned she had dyslexia. This diagnosis helped her understand why she was fearful of reading out loud and why she was unable to read to her first-born son, Timothy, Although Cheryl was challenged with a learning disability, it did not hinder her from pursuing a career in Early  Childhood Education where she became a preschool teacher. That is where the inspiration began. After years of working at a learning center, Cheryl's confidence increased, and the fear of reading dispelled and the gift of writing came alive in her. Cheryl is a strong believer in God and gives all praises to the Lord, the author and finisher, of her faith.

kevonmymiracleboy5@gmail.com

(860)370-0876

MAXINE D. NUGENT

Founder & CEO

www.Roomtobreathect.com
(860) 478-7204
Roomtobreathe1020@gmail.com

We help individuals find comfort in their homes, through planning and organization, by redefining their spaces, adding function and practicality. Our clients are left stress-free, with a peace of mind through our downsizing and decluttering services.

Home Organization

Whether you want to organize a closet, your office or your entire home, I will be there to help you. Do you feel overwhelmed by the clutter in your home? That seems like the norm to a lot of people now-a-days. If you are looking for a Professional Organizer, consider the help of a home and office organization service. The process of decluttering can be so very overwhelming, and at times it may even seem impossible. We will sit and make a plan regarding the process of making organizing work.

Closet Organization

I help you declutter your unorganized space in the closet. By helping you go through your closet and making different boxes for items in your closet. This will make your home more peaceful, more functional, and more enjoyable that is what I do. I help you find the space in your closet that is needed.

Home Staging

Clean your home inside and out before you stage it, in order to do that you will need my help to declutter, depersonalize, and cut down some furniture to stage your home. Stage your home to show off your closets and storage space. By living a cluttered lifestyle, you will not have the time or space to make your deadlines or achieve your goals. Clutter can distract you, weigh you down and in general it invites chaos into your life.

Granny's Doggie Treats

Claudia Cupe dog got attacked about two years ago and he need surgery. Once he got home eating the kibble was making him gain weight because he was less active. Once she started making his food and treats, he started losing weight. Claudia bought him back to the Vet for his yearly checkup, the Vet told her whatever she was doing to keep doing it because Wellington aka Wellybelly was in great shape. With that great news Claudia started sharing the treats with family and friends and attended local farmer's markets. All the dogs love Granny's Doggie Treats because it's a healthier choice for their dog.

🌐 Etsy.com/shop/treatsbyclaudiashop

For any inquires please contact:

Hamilton Brown
President

860-778-5135

filth2freshbc@gmail.com

Filth2Fresh Bin Cleaning

@Filth2FreshBinCleaning

Filth 2 Fresh
BIN CLEANING

NONPROFIT

"Generosity is Priceless!"

Naomi Ngoma
Program Director

successthroughprocess@gmail.com

Equpping and Empowering Low to Moderate Income Individuals to Attain Lifelong Success Through the Mastery of the Four Foundations of:

-EDUCATION
-CAREER
-FINANCES
-SOCIAL/PSYCHOLOGICAL DEVELOPMENT

When Destiny Meets Purpose, Inc.

When Destiny Meets Purpose, Inc started as a one day Conference at The Hartford Hotel & Conference Center in East Hartford, CT on Saturday, October 29, 2016 with a mission to: Envelope purpose driven relationships and lifestyles to enhance the social/economic status of single men and women 18 years old and older through Education, Empowerment Sessions, Interactive Exercises and Communication, and also to provide Singles with the Opportunity to engage with each other in a Safe and Positive Environment; Regardless of Race, Status, or Religious Beliefs. The conference was a huge success with an attendance of 75 men and women from various backgrounds. After the conference there were several suggestions made from those that attended and one of those suggestions was to have more conferences and events that will allow singles to engage with each other. After much consideration Savanda Latrece Gasque the Visionary of When Destiny Meets Purpose, Inc. planned more activities, events, conferences, and seminars throughout the year. From 2016 to 2018 When Destiny Meets Purpose, Inc successfully hosted over 17 events, seminars, and conferences. What started as a one-day conference with a vision to be hosted annually, became a 501-c3 Non-profit organization in December 2018, because of the feedback from the attendees that there was a greater need for an organization that would address the concerns of single men and women in the community. When Destiny Meets Purpose, Inc have grown tremendously and continues to create avenues to be inclusive and accessible to as many people as possible. During the pandemic they hosted empowerment sessions via zoom and social media, and more people from different regions were introduced to the   organization, and we were elated to welcome them. When Destiny Meets Purpose, Inc continues to host their annual celebration, seminars, empowerment sessions in person and online, telephone consultations and assessments, and fundraisers throughout the year.

A portion of the proceeds from the events are donated to Gifts Of Love Outreach (GOLO): When Destiny Meets Purpose, Inc Community Outreach Program: to assist low-moderate income individuals and families with the Basic needs of food, clothes, utility/rental assistance, transportation to work (provide bus passes/assistance with gas), emergency shelter placement, backpacks with school supplies for children in school, provide hot meals and bagged lunches throughout the year and during the holidays, and donate gifts to shelters during Christmas.

Current Project: The Swift Transition- Assist Underserved Individuals and Families in East Windsor, CT with Basic Needs and Food Assistance from June-November. Follow-by Case Management to assist those who are unemployed find gainful employment and those who are facing eviction or homeless apply for affordable Housing.

When Destiny Meets Purpose, Inc Future Endeavors is to open a Swift Transition Home that will assist individuals and families that are homeless with a place to stay for 6 months and provide them with the necessary resources to find gainful employment, reliable transportation, and stable housing. more people from different regions were introduced to the organization, and we were elated to welcome them.

Savanda La'trece

destinymeetspurpose@gmail.com

(860)804-2363

CT Black Owned Businesses Directory Volume 2 will be Available in December 2023 If you would like you would like your business to be in the Directory, please e-mail Info to: destinymeetspurpose@gmail.com or call (860)804-2363

For a 1-page Ad for $30 which would include a Picture of the Business Owner(s), a short bio, the business logo, and business info, in addition you will receive a copy of the Directory at our CT Black Owned Business Celebration in December (Date, Time, and Location TBD)

Business Name:
Address:
Phone#
Email:
Website:

Business Name:
Address:
Phone#
Email:
Website:

Business Name:
Address:
Phone#
Email:
Website:

Business Name:
Address:
Phone#
Email:
Website:

Business Name:
Address:
Phone#
Email:
Website:

Business Name:
Address:
Phone#
Email:
Website: